What's the Issue?

WHAT ARE POLITICAL PARTIES?

By Joyce Jeffries

KidHaven
PUBLISHING

Published in 2019 by
KidHaven Publishing, an Imprint of Greenhaven Publishing, LLC
353 3rd Avenue
Suite 255
New York, NY 10010

Designer: Andrea Davison-Bartolotta
Editor: Katie Kawa

Photo credits: Cover (bottom) JEFF KOWALSKY/AFP/Getty Images; cover (top), p. 5 (main) Hill Street Studios/Blend Images/Getty Images; p. 5 (both insets) Chip Somodevilla/Getty Images; p. 7 (both) Stock Montage/Getty Images; pp. 8, 10 vectorfusionart/Shutterstock.com; pp. 9 (all insets), 11 (all insets) courtesy of the Library of Congress; p. 9 (background) keksik97/Shutterstock.com; p. 11 (background) VectorPic/Shutterstock.com; p. 12 Hulton Archive/Getty Images; p. 13 Scott Olson/Getty Images; p. 15 (top) Mike Coppola/Getty Images; p. 15 (bottom) Tasos Katopodis/ Getty Images; p. 16 Microgen/Shutterstock.com; p. 17 Yellow Dog Productions/Iconica/Getty Images; p. 19 Joshua Roberts/Bloomberg via Getty Images; p. 21 Stephanie Zieber/ Shutterstock.com.

Cataloging-in-Publication Data

Names: Jeffries, Joyce.
Title: What are political parties? / Joyce Jeffries.
Description: New York : KidHaven Publishing, 2019. | Series: What's the issue? | Includes glossary and index.
Identifiers: ISBN 9781534528130 (pbk.) | ISBN 9781534528154 (library bound) | ISBN 9781534528147 (6 pack) | ISBN 9781534528161 (ebook)
Subjects: LCSH: Political parties–United States–Juvenile literature. | Two-party systems–United States–Juvenile literature. | United States–Politics and government–Juvenile literature.
Classification: LCC JK2265.J44 2019 | DDC 324.273–dc23

Printed in the United States of America

CPSIA compliance information: Batch #BW19KL: For further information contact Greenhaven Publishing LLC, New York, New York at 1-844-317-7404.

Please visit our website, www.greenhavenpublishing.com. For a free color catalog of all our high-quality books, call toll free 1-844-317-7404 or fax 1-844-317-7405.

CONTENTS

Political Points of View

Many people have strong feelings about the government. These strong feelings can lead to respectful **debates** or cause arguments when people disagree. This sometimes happens between people from different political parties—groups whose members have the same general beliefs about how the government should work.

In the United States, the **division** between members of different political parties has become a big problem. However, it's one that can be fixed through **cooperation** and respect. When people from different political parties work together, they can learn from each other and help make their country a better place.

Facing the Facts 🔍

A 2018 study showed that more than 70 percent of Americans belong to a political party because they believe their party's plans are good for the United States.

Republican Party

Democratic Party

The two main political parties in the United States are the Republican Party—also known as the Republicans—and the Democratic Party—also known as the Democrats. Understanding both parties is an important part of being an informed, or educated, citizen.

5

Looking Back

Political parties have existed for hundreds of years. In the United States, people were **divided** about how the country should be run before it was even an independent nation. The earliest divide was between the Federalists, who supported a strong national government, and the Anti-Federalists, who opposed this idea. The Anti-Federalists were also known as the Democratic-Republicans.

Although political parties were around before George Washington became the first president of the United States, he wasn't an official member of a party. In fact, he warned Americans about the danger of political parties and the divisions they can cause.

Facing the Facts 🔍

George Washington's most famous warning about political parties was given in his 1796 farewell address, which he gave after deciding not to run for another term as president.

In the late 1700s, Alexander Hamilton (right) was one of the leading Federalists, and Thomas Jefferson (left) led the Democratic-Republicans. Their debates about the powers of the federal, or national, government continue in the United States today.

The Democratic Party

Throughout U.S. history, different political parties have gained and lost power. However, the main divide between people who support a strong central government and people who oppose it has remained.

Today, the Democratic Party supports a strong central government. Democrats generally want a federal government that has power over businesses and the **economy**. In addition, they believe the U.S. government should create **programs** to help the poor and other groups. Since the 1960s, many Democrats have also fought for civil rights for all Americans.

Facing the Facts 🔍

The Democratic Party is often **represented** by the color blue or a picture of a donkey.

Famous Democratic Presidents

name		years in office
Andrew Jackson		1829 to 1837
Franklin D. Roosevelt		1933 to 1945
John F. Kennedy		1961 to 1963
Bill Clinton		1993 to 2001
Barack Obama		2009 to 2017

Many famous U.S. presidents have been members of the Democratic Party. These are just some of them. This political party changed a lot from the time of Andrew Jackson to the time of Barack Obama!

The Republican Party

The Democratic Party is the oldest political party in the United States, but the Republican Party has been around for more than 100 years, too. This party is also known as the Grand Old Party, or GOP.

Unlike Democrats, Republicans generally don't like the idea of a strong central government. They believe in giving most of the power to state and local governments. The Republican Party also fights for lower taxes and for less government control over businesses. In general, the Republican Party supports more **traditional** views of marriage, women's rights, and other social issues than the Democratic Party.

Facing the Facts 🔍

The Republican Party is often represented by the color red or a picture of an elephant.

Famous Republican Presidents

name		years in office
Abraham Lincoln		1861 to 1865
Theodore Roosevelt		1901 to 1909
Ronald Reagan		1981 to 1989
George W. Bush		2001 to 2009
Donald Trump		2017 to present

Shown here are some of the most famous Republican presidents. In the 2016 presidential election, Republican Donald Trump **defeated** Democrat Hillary Clinton to become president.

Third Parties

The United States has a two-party system, which means the Democrats and Republicans have all the power in U.S. politics. However, that doesn't mean other parties don't exist in the United States. In fact, many other parties, called third parties, have been created throughout U.S. history.

Today, two of the most well-known third parties are the Libertarian Party and the Green Party. The Libertarian Party fights for individual rights and against a powerful government. The Green Party fights for the **environment**. In addition, some people don't belong to any political party. They're called independents.

Facing the Facts

Victoria Woodhull—the first woman to run for president of the United States—was a member of a third party. She ran for president in 1872 as a member of the Equal Rights Party.

Third-party presidential **candidates**, such as those shown here, generally know they won't win an election, but they hope to raise awareness for issues that matter to members of their party.

Running for President

Political parties are most often in the news every four years, which is when U.S. presidential elections are held. In some states, members of the Democratic Party and the Republican Party vote for the presidential candidate they want to represent their party in elections called primaries. The candidate who wins the most primaries often represents their party in the general presidential election.

In a presidential election, many Americans vote for the candidate from their political party. However, voters don't have to do this. If they like a candidate from another party, they're free to vote for that candidate.

Facing the Facts 🔍

In some states, members of a political party hold a caucus to choose the presidential candidate they want to represent their party. This is a kind of meeting in which a group makes a decision together.

In presidential election years, the Democratic Party and Republican Party hold national conventions, which are often shown on television. At these conventions, leaders give speeches and vote on the party's platform, or what the party stands for. They also name the party's official presidential candidate.

2016 Republican National Convention

15

In the News

Political news is very popular, and many television channels, magazines, and websites report this kind of news. Many news **sources** try not to favor one political party over another in their reporting. However, some news sources report stories in a way that makes one political party look good while putting down another party.

How can people make sure they're getting a fair and balanced look at all political parties and the leaders of those parties? They can learn more about where their news comes from and get their news from more than one source.

Facing the Facts 🔍

In a 2017 study, 72 percent of Americans said they believe news sources favor one political party over another in their reporting.

Many people like getting their news from a source that shares their political point of view. However, this mean they're often not getting the whole story. It's good to learn about different political parties and their ideas to get a balanced view of the news.

Working Together

News sources aren't the only things that seem to be divided along political party lines in the United States. Many people think political beliefs are pushing Americans farther apart. People from different political parties sometimes get into arguments, and they sometimes say unkind things to each other online, too. Even government leaders sometimes refuse to work with leaders from another political party.

However, many Americans believe people from different political parties should work together. These Americans know that the things they have in common are more important than their political differences.

Facing the Facts

As of 2017, around 80 percent of Democrats and Republicans had a negative, or bad, opinion of members of the other party.

Although Democratic and Republican leaders don't often get along, they sometimes work together to help Americans. When they do this, it's called a bipartisan effort.

19

A More United Country

News stories and online posts can make it seem impossible for members of different political parties to get along. However, that's not the case. Many family members, friends, and coworkers belong to different political parties. They may have different opinions about the government, but they still respect each other.

The political party a person belongs to is only one part of who they are. Taking the time to learn about why a person belongs to a political party helps Americans understand each other better. When that happens, the United States becomes an even more united country.

Facing the Facts 🔍

A 2017 study showed that 54 percent of Americans believe their leaders should work together—no matter what political party they belong to.

WHAT CAN YOU DO?

Learn more about different political parties so you can be a more informed citizen.

Treat people with respect, even if you don't agree with them.

Talk to people you know about their political beliefs, and listen respectfully when they explain why they belong to a certain political party.

Pay attention to primaries, caucuses, and conventions during a presidential election year to learn more about how they work.

Check the sources of the news stories you see to make sure you're getting a balanced look at the world.

Even people who are too young to vote can do their part to make the world a less divided place. These are just some of the ways you can get started!

GLOSSARY

candidate: A person who runs in an election.

cooperation: The act of working with others to get something done.

debate: An argument or discussion about an issue, generally between two sides.

defeat: To win a victory over someone.

divide: To separate into different groups. Also, a separation of people into different groups, often based on different beliefs or opinions.

division: Separation.

economy: The way in which goods and services are made, sold, and used in a country or area.

environment: The natural world around us.

program: A plan under which action may be taken toward a goal.

represent: To act officially or stand for someone or something.

source: A person, place, or thing from which something comes or where it can be found.

traditional: Following what's been done for a long time.

FOR MORE INFORMATION

WEBSITES

Congress for Kids: Political Parties

www.congressforkids.net/Elections_politicalparties.htm

This website gives visitors a basic look at what political parties are and provides links to more information about primaries, conventions, and elections.

Timeline Guide to the U.S. Presidents

www.scholastic.com/teachers/articles/teaching-content/timeline-guide-us-presidents/

Visitors to this website can discover fun facts about each U.S. president, including what political party they belonged to.

BOOKS

Bjornlund, Lydia, and Richard Bell. *Modern Political Parties.* Minneapolis, MN: Core Library, 2016.

Houser, Grace. *Understanding U.S. Elections and the Electoral College.* New York, NY: PowerKids Press, 2018.

McCabe, Matthew. *12 Things to Know About Political Parties.* North Mankato, MN: 12-Story Library, 2015.

Publisher's note to educators and parents: Our editors have carefully reviewed these websites to ensure that they are suitable for students. Many websites change frequently, however, and we cannot guarantee that a site's future contents will continue to meet our high standards of quality and educational value. Be advised that students should be closely supervised whenever they access the Internet.

INDEX